Martin O'Neil: A Brilliant Irish Manager

(A Look Into His Career)

By

Bobby Michaelson

Table of Contents

Preface

Northern Irish professional football manager and former midfielder Martin Hugh Michael O'Neill were born on March 1, 1952.

O'Neill came to England after a brief early career in the Irish League and spent the majority of his playing career with Nottingham Forest. He won the European Cup twice, in 1979 and 1980, and the First Division championship in 1977–1978. He received 64 national team football caps for Northern Ireland, and he also led the squad at the 1982 World Cup.

Grantham Town, Wycombe Wanderers, Norwich City, Leicester City, Celtic, Aston Villa, and Sunderland are among the teams O'Neill has managed. Three times, with two victories, he led Leicester City to the Football League Cup final. He guided Celtic to seven victories while serving as manager from 2000 to 2005, including three Scottish Premier League crowns and the 2003 UEFA Cup Final. He led Aston Villa to the 2010 Football League Cup Final after helping them finish sixth in the English Premier League three times in a row.

In 2013, he was appointed manager of the Republic of Ireland, and in 2016, he guided the team to its third-ever qualification for the UEFA European Championship by defeating Germany.

In November 2018, he and his partner Roy Keane parted ways by "mutual consent." He was hired as the manager of Nottingham Forest in January 2019 but quit after six months.

Childhood and Irish Football Career

In 1952, O'Neill was born in County Londonderry, Northern Ireland's Kilrea. He has four brothers and four sisters and was the sixth of nine children. Pádraig Pearse's Kilrea, a local GAA club, was founded by O'Neill's father. In addition to being on the Derry senior side that won the 1958 Ulster Championship and advanced to that year's All-Ireland Championship final, his brothers Gerry and Leo also played for the club. He also participated in youth play with Derry and Kilrea. When boarding at St. Columb's College in Derry and afterward at St. Malachy's College in Belfast, he also participated in Gaelic football.

He originally gained notoriety as a football player when a student at St. Malachy's, first with the neighborhood team Rosario and later with Distillery. This was against the GAA's rule on Gaelic football players participating in "foreign sports." The Antrim GAA County Council declined to permit St. Malachy played in the 1970 MacRory Cup final at Belfast's Casement Park. To allow him to play, the interested colleges changed the location to County Tyrone. The game was won by St. Malachy's.

Club Career

O'Neill played for the South Belfast team Rosario before joining Distillery in the Irish League. (Today, the neighborhood youth club of Rosario Football Club has a conference room named in his honor.) He won the Irish Cup in 1971 while playing for Distillery, defeating Derry City 3-0 and scoring twice in the process. His second goal, which was scored after a particularly brilliant mazy run in which he dribbled past three opponents, was extremely impressive. Distillery qualified for Europe the next season as a result of winning the cup. In a 3-1 home loss to Barcelona in the European Cup Winners' Cup in September 1971, O'Neill scored.

A Nottingham Forest scout noticed him during this time. In October 1971, after leaving Distillery and giving up his studies at the university, he joined Nottingham Forest.

Nottingham Forest

O'Neill later played a crucial part in Forest's heyday. On November 13, 1971, the club defeated West Bromwich Albion 4-1, and he scored on the occasion. He continued to play in the league that year, making a total of 17 games and tallying twice, although he was unable to stop his team's relegation from the First Division in 1972. Yet when Brian Clough was hired as manager in January 1975, it was the start of a change for Nottingham Forest. O'Neill played a key role in Forest's promotion to the first flight in 1977, their League Cup victory the following year, and their league title the year after that under Clough's leadership.

In 1979, when Forest defeated Malmö in the first round of the European Cup, he was demoted to the bench of replacements after failing to fully recover from an injury. Nevertheless, he took part in their victory over Hamburg in 1980.

Later in Life

O'Neill, paid £250,000 to join Norwich City in February 1981. However, on the final day of the season, Norwich was demoted, and O'Neill used a release clause that allowed him to join Manchester City.

Despite a promising beginning, he quickly lost the manager's favor, and in February 1982, he returned to Norwich, where he scored six goals to help them finish third and gain promotion. He spent one more season at Norwich before moving back to Nottingham to play for Notts County, a team that had multiple relegations.

In 1984, O'Neill tried to make a comeback with Chesterfield, but he was forced to leave the game after 20 minutes due to a knee injury. To stay in shape for the 1986 World Cup team from Northern Ireland, this was created.

O'Neill was invited to join the team by Ray Harford, the manager of Fulham at the time after O'Neill left Chesterfield to get fit again. O'Neill was only able to play in two Fulham reserve games, neither of which he finished, before retiring in February 1985 as a result of a cruciate ligament injury.

World-wide Career

O'Neill made his debut for his nation in a friendly matchup with Scotland at The Oval in February 1971. On October 13, 1971, he then made his senior debut against the Soviet Union national football team in a UEFA Euro 1972 qualification match. As a regular for Northern Ireland, he led the team to the second round of the 1982 World Cup in Spain, when they defeated the hosts in Valencia. From 1971 and 1984, he appeared in 64 games and scored eight goals for Northern Ireland. As a player, he twice won the British Home Championship in 1980 and 1984.

Managerial Career

O'Neill worked at an insurance firm after his playing days before starting a career in football management, initially at Grantham Town in 1987. Then Shepshed Charterhouse's leadership was held there for a limited time after that.

Wolves of Wycombe

In February 1990, he took over as Wycombe Wanderers' manager. In the final game held at Loakes Park, he and George Best both played for the Martin O'Neill XI. He led Wycombe to fifth place in the Football Conference during the 1990–91 season. He guided Wycombe to second place in the Conference during the 1991–92 campaign, falling just short of Colchester United on goal differential.

He led Wycombe into the Football League for the first time the following year. He led Wycombe to a second consecutive promotion in the 1993–94 season via the Division 3 playoffs, and a 4–2 victory over Preston North End sent them into Division 2. Wycombe nearly missed the Division 2 play-offs in the 1994–95 season, and on June 13, 1995, he departed the team to take the helm at Norwich City. O'Neill also won the FA Trophy in 1991 and 1993 while playing for Wycombe.

Wycombe also made it to the Conference League Cup final twice when O'Neill was in charge (winners in 1991–92). The group triumphed in the (Evening Standard) London Fives in 1994 and 1995 as well as three Conference Shield championships. Wycombe lost in the finals of both the Drinkwise Cup and the Berks & Bucks Senior Cup.

He continues to be Wycombe's most successful manager in the club's history as of June 2019.

Norwich City

Due to disagreements with club chairman Robert Chase over the probable acquisition of striker Dean Windass, O'Neill departed Norwich City in December 1995. Before that, O'Neill managed Hull City for £750,000.

Leicester City

After leaving Norwich City, O'Neill promptly joined Leicester City. Leicester was promoted via the playoffs from the Football League to the Premier League in his first season. During his leadership, they won the Football League Cup in 1997, and

2000, and advanced to the competition's final in 1999.

In the Premier League, they placed tenth in 1997, ninth in 1998, ninth in 1999 and eighth in 2000. In 1997–98 and 2000–01, they were eligible for the UEFA Cup thanks to their two League Cup victories.

He was the favorite to become Leeds United's new manager in October 1998.

For his debut game in command, George Graham, who had just left Leeds, brought his Spurs team to Filbert Street. Thousands of "Don't Go Martin" posters were printed by Leicester Mercury as part of a protest, and supporters held them aloft throughout Leicester's victory. Moreover, thousands of balloons were let loose. O'Neill managed Leicester till the end of his contract.

Celtic

O'Neill departed Leicester on June 1st, 2000,
replacing the duo of John Barnes and Kenny
Dalglish to coach Celtic, who had finished second to
Old Firm rivals Rangers in both of their previous
seasons; in the most recent campaign, they had
finished 21 points off the pace of the champions.

O'Neill played in his debut Old Firm match against
Rangers in late August 2000, and Celtic won 6-2.
Since the 1957 Scottish League Cup Final, they had
defeated Rangers more convincingly than ever
before. Nevertheless, things turned around in his
second Old Firm match when Celtic lost 5-1.

O'Neill won a domestic treble with Celtic in that
inaugural season, the first time this had been done
since 1968–1969. At that time, Alex Ferguson, who

had declared his intention to quit Manchester United in 2002, was seen as a possible successor. The league championship was then retained by Celtic in 2001–02, marking the first time since 1982 that Celtic had accomplished that feat. Celtic, who won all of their home games but dropped all of their away games, also advanced to the Champions League group stage.

He later led Celtic to the 2003 UEFA Cup Final in Seville, where they lost to a José Mourinho-coached Porto team 3-2 in extra time.

Celtic defeated Blackburn, Celta Vigo, Stuttgart, Liverpool, and Boavista en route to their first European championship since 1970. Celtic overcame rival Rangers to win the league title the next year and advanced to the UEFA Cup quarterfinals, where they defeated Barcelona.

Celtic announced that O'Neill would step down as manager on May 25 to care for his wife Geraldine, who had lymphoma. On May 28, 2005, Alan Thompson's goal in the eleventh minute gave Celtic the 1-0 victory over Dundee United in the Scottish Cup final, his final competitive game as Celtic's manager.

Celtic played 282 games under O'Neill, winning 213, drawing 29, and losing 40. O'Neill was the most successful Celtic manager since Jock Stein. O'Neill won three League championships, three Scottish Cups, and a League Cup during his five seasons at Celtic Park. He lost the two league championships by a goal or a point. He also oversaw Celtic's achievement of a British record of 25 straight league victories in the 2003–04 season, as well as a record 7 consecutive victories in Old Firm derbies. His win percentage of 75.5% is the highest in club history for a manager.

Aston Villa

On August 4, 2006, O'Neill was presented as the Aston Villa manager during a press conference. He said at the press conference;

"Being back, being a part of this club is truly great. This presents an excellent challenge. I am very familiar with this football team's past. Though attempting to return it to its former splendor seems far-fetched, why not give it a shot? They haven't won the European Cup in almost 25 years, but it is still the goal."

In the Premier League in 2006–07, Villa had the longest streak of games without a loss (9 games), without dropping a match until 28 October. After a midseason downturn, Villa rallied late in the year, winning three of their away matches in April, to finish the year with a run of nine unbeaten games. O'Neill won the title of Premier League Manager of the Month for April as a result. Villa finished 11th, up 5 spots from the previous season, with a final point total of 50, an improvement of 8 over the previous campaign.

Randy Lerner, the owner of Aston Villa, declared in October 2007 that if O'Neill received an offer to coach England, he would not prevent O'Neill from leaving Villa. Afterward, O'Neill denied the reports, referring to them as "unfair speculation."

On the last day of the 2007–08 campaign, Aston Villa narrowly missed out on a UEFA Cup spot and, by placing sixth, earned a spot in the Intertoto Cup. They were the third-top goal scorers with 71 goals, which was their best total in the Premier League since winning the championship in 1981. Villa also recorded 60 points, which was their biggest total since 1996–97.

After 25 games of the 2008-09 season, the club was third in the table with 51 points, 2 points ahead of Chelsea on equal games, 7 points ahead of Arsenal in fifth place, and on track to qualify for the Champions League for the first time since 1983. They also qualified for the UEFA Cup as joint winners of the Intertoto Cup. O'Neill decided to put Champions League qualification first and fielded essentially a backup team for a UEFA Cup match against CSKA Moscow, which they ultimately lost. Following this, Villa lost all eight of its subsequent league contests, and due to Arsenal and Chelsea's improved play, Villa was unable to finish in the top four.

While Villa did not initially advance to the newly renamed Europa League group stage, they did advance in the league with victories over Manchester United, Chelsea, and Liverpool.

Arsenal drew at home and defeated Villa 3-0 at Emirates Stadium.

Villa once again improved their points total, finishing with 64 points for the third season in a row, but their poor home form (they drew 8 times at home) prevented them from having a shot at making the UEFA Champions League.

On February 28, 2010, Aston Villa faced Manchester United in the League Cup final; it was their first final under Martin O'Neill and they're first in 10 years. Nevertheless, they fell short 2-1.

O'Neill left his position as Aston Villa manager effective immediately on August 9, 2010. As he left, O'Neill said,

"My time at Aston Villa has been fantastic. It must be difficult to leave such a beautiful club."

Although O'Neill had issues with the transfer budget, the club and its players were nevertheless taken aback by his abrupt departure just five days before the start of the new season. Two days later, Lerner said in a statement that while they "no longer had a common view as to how to move ahead," they "remain dear friends."

Sunderland

On December 3, 2011, O'Neill agreed to a three-year contract with Sunderland, the Premier League team he had rooted for as a young fan.
Sunderland overcame a 1-0 deficit to defeat Blackburn Rovers 2-1 at the Stadium of Light in

O'Neill's first game in charge. After four victories from his first six games, including one over league-leading Manchester City, Sunderland rapidly improved under O'Neill. The Daily Telegraph suggested that if Sunderland kept up their performance, they might make a late push for a spot in Europe.

During O'Neill's first few months in charge, Sunderland kept up their strong play. They improved to ninth place in the standings and kept up their fight for a Europa League spot. They defeated Arsenal 2-0 on February 18 to advance past them in the FA Cup fifth round. They suffered a 4-0 defeat to West Bromwich Albion a week later. It was O'Neill's first Tyne-Wear derby the following week. The "fiercely contested" game ended in a draw at 1-1, with Sunderland receiving two red cards. The following week at the Stadium of Light, Sunderland defeated Liverpool 1-0. After eight games without a victory, Sunderland's record faltered after the season, but they still managed to finish a respectable 13th, a finish that Sunderland supporters would have been pleased with following the season's early going.

To improve upon his previous 13th-place finish and challenge for the top 10, O'Neill purchased Steven Fletcher and Adam Johnson for the next season. He claimed a convincing 0-0 draw against Arsenal in the season opener at the Emirates. Before a 3-0 loss to Manchester City, Sunderland went undefeated in its first five games. Then, a late Demba Ba own goal helped them earn a 1-1 draw in O'Neill's first Tyne-Wear derby at the Stadium of Light. Then, Sunderland lost unexpectedly at home to Aston Villa 0-1 and to Middlesbrough 1-0 in the League Cup. Following West Brom's 2-4 home loss, there were rumors that O'Neill had resigned. All of these were immediately put to rest, as O'Neill carried on despite entering the relegation zone after losing to Chelsea

1-3 at home. As Sunderland climbed the rankings after an outstanding run of results that included another 1-0 victory over Manchester City and a 2-3 victory over Wigan, their fortunes began to turn around and they reached a season-high of 11th. Unfortunately, Sunderland went 8 games without a win, making this O'Neill's final triumph.

Following a 1-0 loss to Manchester United, which put the team one point above the Premier League relegation zone with seven games remaining in the season, Martin O'Neill was fired by Sunderland on March 30, 2013. Before O'Neill's departure, Sunderland had lost all eight of its games and had only earned three of a possible 24 points during that stretch.

Republic of Ireland

On November 5, 2013, the Republic of Ireland, O'Neill was officially appointed as the team's new manager. Former club captain Roy Keane joined him as his assistant manager. On November 15, 2013, he won his debut game in charge 3-0 against Latvia at the Aviva Stadium. In O'Neill's first away match as manager, on November 19, 2013, the team drew 0-0 with Poland at the Stadion Miejski in Pozna. On March 5, 2014, he suffered his first managerial defeat, a 2-1 friendly loss to Serbia at home.

The Republic of Ireland defeated Bosnia and Herzegovina 3-1 on aggregate in the play-offs to advance to UEFA Euro 2016 on November 16, 2015.

Following remarks that were deemed to be sexist about the physical attributes of players' female partners, O'Neill courted controversy in March

2016. There is no place for remarks of this sort in Irish football, especially at this level, according to Orla O'Connor of the National Women's Council of Ireland.

O'Neill extended his contract on June 7, 2016, through the 2018 FIFA World Cup in Russia.

Ireland won 1-0 against Italy on June 22, 2016, to finish first in their Euro 2016 group and advance to face France in the round of 16.

O'Neill faced backlash in June 2016 after he used a pejorative phrase to refer to LGBT persons. O'Neill told a group of Ireland football fans during a public appearance in Cork that month that he had two others travel with assistant Roy Keane and him on a previous trip to San Francisco because he was concerned people could believe they were "queers." He was urged to apologize to the LGBT community by the Gay and Lesbian Equality Network (GLEN), which denounced the remarks. The National LGBT Federation also urged O'Neill to retract his comments and apologize, pointing out that his actions may only undermine efforts to combat homophobic bias in sports. A few days later, he expressed regret for the offensive statement.

Ireland defeated Wales 1-0 on October 9 to go to the qualification play-offs.

On November 11, Ireland and Denmark played to a scoreless draw in Copenhagen during the first leg of the playoffs. Ireland took the lead in the game before falling to Denmark 5-1 in the second leg on November 14 in Dublin. O'Neill informally agreed to the term in October 2017 and then inked a new two-year contract with the FAI in January 2018.

On their UEFA Nations League debut against Wales on September 6, 2018, an undermanned Ireland fell 4-1.

Ireland eventually placed last in their group, earning just two points from two goalless draws with Denmark, and was demoted to UEFA Nations League C for the 2020–21 season (although were later restored to League B following a format change).

On November 21, 2018, O'Neill and the FAI parted ways.

<u>Nottingham Forest</u>

On January 15, 2019, it was revealed that O'Neill had been appointed as Nottingham Forest's manager. The club finished the Championship in ninth position under O'Neill's leadership. On June 28,

2019, not long after his assistant Roy Keane left the team, he was fired as manager.

Outside of Football

O'Neill never finished his degree yet he still believes
in criminology. The 1961 James Hanratty case
sparked his interest.

For the World Cup, the European Championship,
and UEFA Champions League games, he worked as
an analyst for BBC and ITV.

O'Neill cheered for Celtic F.C. and Sunderland
A.F.C. in his boyhood. Charlie Hurley, the center-
back and captain of Sunderland, was his favorite
player and finally received the club's Man of the
Century award in 1979.

For his contributions to association of football,
O'Neill was named a Member of the Order of the
British Empire (MBE) in the 1983 New Year

Honours and elevated to Officer of the same Order (OBE) in the 2004 New Year Honours.

He was elected into the Norwich club's Hall of Fame in 2002 by the club's fans.

On November 3, 2013, he received the Nottingham Lifetime Achievement Award in recognition of his contributions to football and successes with Nottingham Forest.

Two daughters were born to O'Neill and his wife Geraldine.

Honors

Player

1970–1971: Nottingham Forest Irish Cup

1977–1978: First Division

League Cup (1977–1978 and 1978–1979)

1978–1979: European Cup, 1979–80

1978: FA Charity Shield

1979: European Super Cup

1976–1977: Anglo–Scottish Cup

Ireland, Northern

1979–1980: British Home Championship

As Manager of Wycombe Wanderers

Playoffs for the Football League's Third Division:
1994

1992–1993: Football Conference

FA Cup: 1990–91 and 1992–93

1991–1992 Conference League Cup

Football Conference Championship: 1991–1992,
1992–1993, and 1993–1994

Leicester City

1996 Football League First Division Playoffs

Football League Cup winners in 1996–97 and 1999–
2000

Celtic

Scottish Premier League seasons from 2000–2001 to
2003–2004

Scottish Cup winners in 2000-01, 2003-04, and
2004-05

2000–0: Scottish League Cup

Runner-up in the UEFA Cup: 2002–03

Stoke City

2009–2010, Football League Cup runner-up

Individual

—September 1997, October 1998, November 1999, April 2007, November 2007, December 2008, April 2010, and December 2011 were all Premier League Manager of the Month.

—August 2000, December 2000, February 2001, August 2001, April 2002, November 2002, October 2003, November 2003, and January 2005: Scottish Premier League Manager of the Month

—LMA 1993–1994: Football League First Division Manager of the Year.
—LMA 1995–1996: Football League Third Division Manager of the Year.
—Manager of the Year for the SFWA in 2000, 2001, and 2003.

—2003–2004 Scottish Premier League Manager of the Year.

A Review of On Days Like These

In the Republic of Ireland, rumors regarding Martin O'Neill's autobiography have already started to circulate. Keith Andrews, Stephen Kenny's assistant with Ireland, is the final target of On Days Like These, a book that spans five decades in football. When he was excoriatingly critical of me on television, Stephen's lieutenant "found himself in a hotter seat in the dugout than the one he sat in a TV studio," O'Neill writes.

The 70-year-old is perfectly aware of what the response entailed. In the course of a lengthy chat in a London hotel, O'Neill states, "I'm "bitter." I'm not permitted to defend myself, then? Nobody enjoys criticism, but I believe I have handled it rather effectively during my career.

The way Andrews fits into O'Neill's line of work is what jars. As O'Neill puts it,

I could disagree if Roy Keane was doing punditry work and said I'd made a mess of something, but I would accept it from someone who has played at that level, has managed himself, and knows the demands you are under.

I have a certain amount of deserved respect for that viewpoint, but not as much as a lower-leaguer who has never experienced winning a medal. And who is currently discovering how challenging it is to win football games?

It is challenging. Even now, Alex Ferguson would be worried about traveling to Southampton and succeeding. So you can imagine what it may be like when you are, for the most part, competing against stronger opponents at the international level.

O'Neill's five-year international stint and his interactions with the Irish football media continue to be fascinating.

It would be inaccurate to portray O'Neill's memoir as a means of settling scores, as some have claimed. There is the occasional bit of sarcasm—after all, one would expect nothing less—but the incredible career that reached its peak as a player under Brian Clough before reaching managerial brilliance at Celtic and Leicester is shown in a lighthearted manner. The entire thing is self-deprecating.

O'Neill still clearly recalls a "mesmeric" Clough from the moment of their first encounter in the winter of 1975. O'Neill was elevated to the first team right away by Clough, who was not in the mood to coo.

"Hey, you: Quit putting your partner through hell. In an early training session, the instructor said, "You look like a boy who would put your partner in the shit."

Those engaged in Nottingham Forest's legendary run were unaware of how much history was being made both domestically and overseas. The ride was you, O'Neill explains. "In contrast to last year, when beating Bristol Rovers was difficult, you go to West Ham expecting to win. We probably didn't realize it was exceptional until after it was finished. Oh, that's it, you thought the night we lost to the Bulgarians [CSKA Sofia in 1980] in the European Cup.

For a complex individual, he engaged in a very straightforward game. He was a master of strategy, but that's not how others view him. He is seen as a shouter, a motivator, or a charmer. He was an expert at the game. He provided us with timeless tactical advice while playing games. On a Monday, he would tell you one thing, then on a Friday, he would contradict himself, and you would believe both.

Billy Bingham's decision to name O'Neill the first Catholic captain of Northern Ireland was extremely audacious at the beginning of the 1980s. O'Neill remembers Billy saying, "We achieve the results, everything will take care of itself." And so it did.

Early on, I would have faced some criticism for my decision, but not nearly as much as Billy did. He never mentioned it to me or indicated that it troubled him. When he could have avoided me and had a simpler life, he was willing to take a chance.

O'Neill recognizes the irony of feeling like a "northerner" or an "outsider" when he assumed leadership of the Republic. Press relations were strained on an ongoing basis.

I believe they thought I had a certain amount of vanity and arrogance about myself. It simply didn't work, practically right away.

With a team that no objective observer could logically characterize as outstanding, O'Neill led Ireland to the round of 16 at Euro 2016. Another World Cup hope was crushed a year later by a Christian Eriksen-inspired Denmark team. O'Neill was surprised by what he encountered. He claims,

I deserve criticism. But, it was a complete outpouring. The doors unlocked. It was a World Cup playoff game for the group we finished fourth in.

Keane, who left Ipswich in 2011, has not managed since, and O'Neill is effusive in his appreciation of him. O'Neill's youth coach at Forest, Bert Johnson, gave Keane some advice that he thinks is relevant.

You have a reputation as an early riser and may spend the entire day in bed, he claims.

A motivation, a driving force, things become buried. Roy Keane can eloquently discuss the sport. When he was last considered for the Sunderland position, I was hoping he would accept it because I believe he would make an excellent manager. Would using techniques be problematic? Without a doubt. He truly has a contribution to make.

Before becoming a household name for Glasgow's green side, O'Neill had excelled in Wycombe and Leicester. In his book, he recounts the shocking incident of having his wife and kid ejected from a hotel room outside of the city before an Old Firm game on the rather dubious pretext that the Rangers squad was staying there. Yet, he normally enjoyed the goldfish bowl, which was uncommon for someone in that setting. He describes it as "a tremendous rivalry between two unbelievable clubs." I'm not being sycophantic by leaving out the Rangers from that. I loved the competition. I cherished the conflict. Whilst there was occasionally an overwhelming feeling and you searched for relief, it had a brutally bright quality.

Previously, O'Neill wanted to lead Aston Villa into the Champions League. It was ended by a deterioration in the relationship between Randy Lerner, the manager, and the owner. O'Neill alleges that Lerner changed his mind after agreeing to bring Scott Parker to Villa and keep James Milner despite Manchester City's £24 million overtures. Earlier, O'Neill had a brief conversation with renowned Villa goalkeeper Doug Ellis, who chastised the Irishman for substituting Martin Laursen late in a draw at Arsenal. Ellis was furious about the move since it cost Villa £3,000 in an appearance fee. O'Neill says,

I finished the tea offered to me and reminded him that we have an important game against Reading on Wednesday night.

I might need Martin again, Mr. Chairman, if that's okay with you?

Even if there is a response, I miss it as I exit the room.

O'Neill felt betrayed by what he saw as the abrupt end of his tenure at Sunderland, the team he had admired since he was a young boy. The assertion that the team lacked fitness from Paolo Di Canio, O'Neill's replacement, added salt to the wound. It is insulting to the former manager, therefore I always tried to stay away from it, says O'Neill.

In the summer, he adds roughly 15 new players, and of course, I'm watching from afar. The audience is unhappy because they can't produce results. He was

questioned about physical fitness.

Oh, my fitness is for after Christmas. If you can

make it till Christmas, you're lucky.

A really good football player. Terrific. You could fit all of his managerial knowledge into a thimble. Even though everyone has some form of ego, life can't just be about you.

The O'Neill management chapter that might end there returned to Nottingham. In 2019, he was quickly dumped once more. He explains,

I had declined Forest a few times. I wouldn't have

bothered if someone had told me that I would

receive 19 games. particularly after winning the last

three. All I wanted was 18 months. I would have left

even if I hadn't gotten them up from the

Championship.

O'Neill still has a young body and mind. If his days in the dugout are numbered, he rightfully refuses to accept that fact entirely.

Could I operate at the highest level? Such things don't, in my opinion, leave you. The spirit, the resolve, the passion, and the desire... As I depart this earth, those things will also leave me.

Interviews

Interview with Callum

(The questions asked by the interviewer is in bold format)

Martin O'Neill was the subject of an interview with Callum McFadden.

— To start, I have a question for you regarding Brian Clough and Nottingham Forest. How quickly did Clough manage to change the club after coming on board in 1975?

"During his tenure as Nottingham Forest manager, Brian Clough completely overhauled the organization from top to bottom. But, it wasn't until

Peter Taylor joined Brian to work together that we saw Clough at his best.

He made us into champions of England and back-to-back winners of the European Football Championship from a Second Division team that was battling in the division that you would now call the Championship.

It's difficult to think things will ever occur in the same way in a current game. Despite Brian's obvious charisma, success did not come right away after he arrived. Even though he had progressively shifted his stamp to the side, we started to take off when Taylor arrived as his assistant about 18 months after his arrival."

— In 1979, you took home the First Division crown as well as the League Cup. After that accomplishment, in 1980 and 1981, the European Cup was won back-to-back with a Super Cup

victory in between. Can you pinpoint precisely what it was that Clough and Taylor accomplished that rendered Forest football immortal?

The fact that their strategy was very straightforward was key. Brian Clough was aware of tactics; he never for a moment pretends otherwise. Nonetheless, he did not pay close attention to the opposition. Instead of focusing on the perceived weaknesses of the adversary, everything was planned around how we could harm them. Brian did not belittle talented individuals or groups, but he seldom ever discussed them before a game.

He was usually quite upbeat, and he made sure that we players understood what he was saying. No matter how smart you are as a player, you do not want a dozen instructions to worry about before a game. He never overcomplicated us as players with several messages before a game.

You start to question who should be on the field if a manager gives out too many orders. Everyone on his side understood their responsibilities, and we frequently performed them to the best of our abilities.

— How did Forest's performance on the European stage compare to his performance in the English Premier League?

Callum, that's a good question.

Brian Clough did not change his strategy from playing local football to playing in Europe. Because we did not have fast access to information about players from all leagues and clubs as we do now owing to Google and the like, we occasionally

felt like we were playing specific opponents in the unknown. For instance, Dynamo Berlin was one of our quarter final opponents in the second European Cup victory. Although we were aware that they were a good team, we relied on scouting reports to learn more about them rather than sitting down to view videos of them playing.
It was the only significant distinction between the two competitions.

— The trophies Forest won under Clough speak for themselves, and that group will always be remembered for their success. What were your highlights from that time at the club, given that you were a significant part of it?

Winning the second European Cup, which I participated in because I wasn't injured in the first victory, was my high point.

It is tremendously special to be on the field when the final whistle is blown to declare your team the European champions. The recollection is wonderful.

The semi-final match versus Cologne at the City Stadium stands out as another vivid recollection. It was the most electrifying game I have ever experienced there.
We drew 3-3 on the night, so to go to the final, we had to travel to Germany and triumph there. Fortunately, we were able to do that and go to the final, capping off an outstanding performance in the competition.

— **You played for teams like Norwich City and Manchester City in addition to Forest. Yet because you led your nation at the 1982 World Cup, I want to concentrate on your international career with Northern Ireland. When you reflect, how much does that mean to you?**

It was another amazing moment in my career, but it was also an amazing time for the nation. It was nothing short of incredible for us to defeat the World Cup hosts Spain and advance to the quarterfinals. The fact that Mal Donaghy was sent off and we had to hold on against Spain made the triumph much more memorable for us. It was great, and I still remember that game like it was yesterday since it was so important to everyone at the time.

— **Once you stopped playing football, you entered the management of the sport. Was that the original plan after retirement?**

Not (laughs). Even though I worked with two of the best professors you could want in Clough and Taylor, I was not at all thinking about it. I didn't give it any thought until I ran across Peter Taylor in Nottingham's downtown a few years after

retiring. I was shocked when he predicted that I
would advance to management. I gave it a lot of
thought when I got home that night after he told me
he was upset that I had not entered management
after retiring.

That conversation "resonated with me," thus I
started to apply for open managerial positions at the
time.

**— Your first management position was with
Wycombe Wanderers, which you led out of the
conference and into the Football League while
winning a ton of trophies along the way. How
would you summarize your entire experience at
the club?**

Wycombe was a fantastic period in my career, but it
was also a critically important period because, if I
had failed there, it's likely that I would not have

been given another managing opportunity in football.

Thankfully, everything turned out well for myself and the club, and I can honestly say that during my time in charge, I gave Wycombe my heart and soul.

— You moved on from Wycombe to Norwich City and then Leicester City. You achieve Premier League promotion with Leicester and build on that achievement with two League Cup triumphs at Wembley. What are your favorite memories from that period of your professional life?

When I first arrived at Leicester, we had a bad start. Because it appeared that I was unable to win games, the crowd was in an uproar. Things were really difficult. I believe it took me eight league games to record my first victories, which led me to believe that there was no hope of promotion even at that early point.

Yet thanks to the players and my staff, we fought back and surged forward, achieving our goal of being promoted to the Premier League. I thoroughly enjoyed my time at Leicester, and winning the League Cups was a memorable experience for both the players and the supporters.

If they can forgive those first few months, I hope they remember it fondly" (laughs). Leaving the club was always going to require something spectacular, and Celtic presented the opportunity that was too good to pass up.

— **In 2000, you arrived at Celtic. The season before your arrival, the squad finished 21 points behind the Rangers. As you were thinking about moving to the club, did it worry you in any way?**

Yes! Indeed, it is the answer. Of course, I was worried. I have to be honest. Nothing during the preseason in Germany and Ireland persuaded me otherwise. I held out hope that if I could recruit a few guys, the tide would gradually turn because I had legitimate concerns.

Mark Viduka was a very excellent striker, and I would have been happy if he had stayed at the club. Nevertheless, when he left, I knew I wanted to replace him with Chris Sutton from Chelsea. Truthfully, Chris's signing an impact on our team during my first season was huge. Once he calmed down, he quickly established himself as a key member of the team and a great counterbalance to Henrik Larsson.

Chris and Henrik enjoyed playing together. Chris' addition to the football team gave us the boost we required, as without his signing at the time, we might not have defeated Rangers 6-2 early in the season.

If that hadn't happened, things could have been extremely different. Chris promised me he would never become a pundit, but since we are talking about Chris, I'd like to point out that he is now one (laughs). But even with our lightheartedness, he was fantastic for the club and significantly altered my life.

— **Was the 6-2 victory over Rangers in just your fifth league game as Celtic's manager the first time you felt that you could accomplish something spectacular in your debut campaign?**

At the time, even after that game, I believed it was premature to draw that conclusion. In retrospect, as you and other Celtic supporters have pointed out to me, that might have been the time when the guard changed. Could have been.

Rangers did defeat us 5-1 in November, which was a setback, but even then, I believed that we had developed a collective inner power to get us through any difficulties that could come our way. From then, we went on to defeat our rivals by a margin of 15 points, which was an amazing accomplishment for everyone.

— You achieved a domestic triple with Celtic, becoming the first manager since Jock Stein to do so. In your first season in charge, you did such. Can you express how special that was for you in words?

It was a demanding season, but the club had a fantastic year. When we defeated Kilmarnock in the League Cup final in March of that year, I first began to believe that we could win a treble, or at the very least, be in the running to do so. I believed we could win the Scottish Cup since we were leading the league and had already won our first trophy as a team.

It was amazing that we were able to accomplish it. The beautiful thing about Scotland, though, is that even after winning a treble, you don't have time to reflect on it and revel in your glory since attention is already turned to the upcoming season and whether you can repeat the feat. You know this Callum. In addition to being a satisfying season, it was also mentally taxing for me. I took a little break of about 7 to 10 days to unwind before returning to fully concentrate on the job that would come in the following season.

— **With the signing of players like Chris Sutton, John Hartson, Alan Thompson, and Neil Lennon, Celtic is thought to have a solid recruiting strategy. But you also received Henrik Larsson, Paul Lambert, and Lubomir Moravcik, three**

elite athletes. As a manager, were they nearly like a godsend?

I can honestly say that they felt like a gift from God to me. The best two-footed player I've ever worked with is Lubo Moravcik. Without a doubt. He had no weaker foot and could go in either direction.

He was about 33 years old when I first started working with him. He was such a gifted player that I genuinely believe we would have won the UEFA Cup final against Porto in Seville if he had been around 27 or 28 at the time. Indeed, I am sure of that. He would have doused Seville in all manner of sorcery. I do think that.

Although Porto possessed several excellent players, Lubo was capable of handling any situation and would have presented Derlei and the company with a variety of challenges.

Paul Lambert was a wonderful player who excelled for both Celtic and me as well as for himself. It is nothing short of miraculous to progress from St Mirren and Motherwell to trials in Germany, secure a transfer to Dortmund, and then go on to win a European Cup.

Henrik Larsson, who was nothing short of amazing, comes next. a fantastic goal scorer and all-around football player. He was courageous as a lion and versatile, playing with both Chris Sutton and John Hartson as strike partners.

It is understandable why Celtic supporters hold him in high regard. He is the best there is. The fact that he left Celtic to join Barcelona and play a significant part in their 2006 European Cup victory before playing for Manchester United in his late 30s is pleasing to me.

He demonstrated his ability to perform on the two largest football stages in Europe, La Liga, and the Premier League. an exceptional talent

— How did you, generally speaking, handle the aforementioned prominent players that you had at Celtic? Did you make an effort to make things simpler like Brian Clough had done for you during your playing career?

It's done, Callum. I allowed these players to play. You get it back to you tenfold if you do that. Let them play how they naturally play and create an environment where they can prosper by having enough depth throughout the squad to back them, as I did as well.
Be careful not to overwhelm them with information. There was no need for that. They required support and management, which Sir Alex excelled at

providing at Manchester United for players like Eric

Cantona.

Guys like that must be allowed to play. The rest,

who were better performers, followed in terms of

prizes and success after I succeeded in my goal.

— You left Celtic in 2005 due to family
obligations before joining Aston Villa more than
a year later. During your tenure as manager, you
came so close to advancing the team to the
Champions League. What stands out in your
mind most about your time spent at the Villains?

I had yet another fantastic period in my career.

Getting the team into the Champions League was

my goal.

It was challenging because they had more funds than

we did, including Manchester United under Sir

Alex, Chelsea under Mourinho, and Arsenal under

Wenger.

Despite everything, we continued to aspire for the top four. We came close to winning the UEFA Cup twice, which was fantastic, but we wanted to be in the Champions League. We came very close to defeating Manchester United in the League Cup in 2010, and I think we would have succeeded if the referee hadn't dismissed Nemanja Vidic for a last-man challenge.

We were awarded a penalty, but I think that only a booking was appropriate. Vidic ought to have left because who knows what might have occurred.

Although winning something with Aston Villa would have been nice, the Champions League was the main objective.

— **To qualify for Euro 2016, you led the Republic of Ireland from 2013 to 2018. By appointing Roy Keane as your assistant, you aroused questions. What led to the choice?**

We got to know one another over a few years because ITV had hired Roy to work with them while they were covering the Champions League. We discussed the idea of cooperating should I ever return to management if he was available. We didn't give it much thought beyond that, but when the job in Ireland opened up, I asked Roy to come along, and I was thrilled when he accepted.

Roy was a manager in his way. He was never shy about expressing an opinion, but even when we didn't agree, he would follow my lead. Roy was a pleasure to work with and well-known to the players. He had a positive influence on the team, which was wonderful.

— How did playing versus managing at a significant international competition compare?

That was lovely when we first arrived in France in 2016. When I watched the old film of Jack Charlton leading Ireland in a significant tournament and the scenes that went with it, it was more like a dream. Because the supporters follow the team everywhere, I wanted to recreate some memorable moments for them, and fortunately, we were able to do so during the tournament.

Robbie Brady's courageous headed goal in France, which helped us defeat Italy, was undoubtedly the game's high point. The main difference between managing in such a competition and participating in it was that throughout the weeks leading up to it, you were doing everything you could to create a good team as well as a great environment overall. In contrast, when you're a player, your attention is on your performance and preparation for a tournament. Both of the encounters were wonderful.

— **Last but not least, Martin, you recently published "On Days Like These: My Life in Football," your autobiography. Why do you believe that the time is perfect for the book now? Does this imply that you might not be seen entering the dugout in the future?**

That's a great question. It was fun to write the book, and it gave me a drive and purpose. It was beneficial to look back on them and offer my insights because I had played football for a considerable number of decades.

In all honesty, though, if another opportunity in management presented itself, I would most definitely consider it. I have not actively sought out any opportunities, but if one were to present itself that fit both me and a potential club, I would give it careful consideration. Let's wait and see.

But, I have had a great time playing football, and I have done my best to convey that in the book.

Interview with Brendan

(The questions asked by the interviewer is in bold format)

The former Republic of Ireland and Celtic manager Martin O'Neill speaks with Brendan Crossan, September 2022, on a turbulent and incredibly successful career in football following the publication of his autobiography, "On Days Like These."

Crossan, Brendan: How much time did you spend writing your autobiography?

I first fidgeted with it on my first day as a professional footballer after leaving Belfast, and it increased from there. Thus, I would estimate that it took about six months. Although I had written a lot of it by hand, I later discovered that there were simpler ways to do it. I simply felt that as I wrote it in my long hand, I could nearly hear my voice.

— **Nowadays, not many people publish their novels.**

You're right. I wanted to handle things on my own. I've had offers to have things ghostwritten a few times, but after seeing that some former players don't even read their memoirs, I decided to do it myself at least to get it done. There may have also been a cathartic element to the whole thing.

— **The book contains some exquisitely crafted parts. Which chapter of the book did you most enjoy writing?**

My first day as a professional football player was in late 1971 when I was a student at Queen's University and moved from Distillery. Brian

Clough's arrival in 1975 is something I remember like it was yesterday, therefore I have no trouble recalling either of those events. As a child, I dreamed of being a professional football player for the English League, thus I thoroughly loved writing that section.

— **Growing up, we were neighbors of Jimmy McAlinden, the legendary former Belfast Celtic player and FA Cup champion with Portsmouth. You recount Jimmy's assistance in arranging your first contract in England in your book. He appeared to be a sort of mentor.**

Definitely. Also, even though each of the five or six reserve games I played at Distillery showed growth, I was still a long way from being on the first team.

But Jimmy put me in Portadown's first team. I'll never be able to pay him back. After a goal from me, we triumphed 3-2. He had decided that the time had come, regardless of whether I deserved to be on the first team or not. I never actually turned around either. Jimmy was extremely intelligent and served as a mentor to me during that year.

— Given that you spent five years working for the Republic of Ireland, I had hoped to read more about your managerial career there. Is that an indication that you're not finding it to be as enjoyable as you'd hoped?

The book that followed the Republic of Ireland job doesn't even cover my 19 games with Nottingham Forest. I doubt I expected the Ireland section of the book to be as brief if anything. And I'll remember that. But I enjoyed it. Managing the team was an honor; it was fantastic, and we enjoyed success in France in 2016...

I wanted to mentally recreate—or at the very least, attempt to imitate—Jack Charlton's accomplishment. I thought, "This is exactly what it's all about," when I witnessed over 20,000 Irish fans cheering loudly during our opening match against Sweden in Paris.

Robbie Brady's goal against Italy, which is discussed just as much as Shane Long's goal against Germany, at least gave us a small taste of Jack Charlton's remarkable success.

The truth is that, as you are well aware, I never really clicked with the Irish media and they never really clicked with me. As a result, we never really connected on any level. And even though it was a playoff game to try to qualify for the 2018 World Cup, it's apparent that our loss to Denmark and the crushing defeat we received made things worse. I questioned, "Is it a dismissible offense?" To be frank, I believe I could have handled the press interviews a little bit better.

— **Your media relations had a combative tone, and I'm sure the media weren't entirely to blame. How might you have handled things more effectively?**

I believe I should have given myself a little more time to rest. You are being interviewed right away following a game, whether you won or lost. It's not an issue when you succeed. When you lose, you take criticism without a doubt. So, after Denmark, it was incredibly frustrating, especially after being tied [in the first leg] in Copenhagen.
It appeared from this distance at least that it was a moment they were waiting for to be thoroughly defeated in Dublin. After then, things kind of went south.

I could have taken an extra minute or two to inform the media that we were the fourth seed in our group and that this game was a World Cup play-off. Today's loss to Denmark at home might not seem as awful. We ought to perhaps take a moment to consider how the squad performed. Hey, looking back is an amazing thing.

— You had a fairly small squad with Ireland, but you can't just say, "Oh, we're not very good, are we?"

Seamus Coleman might have been the lone player competing at the time in the Premier League. The most crucial task was to genuinely inspire players to perform as strongly and for as long as possible during the 90 minutes to truly overcome obstacles— obstacles posed by facing superior teams. There were several Championship players on the side. I'm proud of myself for even getting to the 2016 Euros.

My task was not to fix the League of Ireland's problems or anything of the sort. My sole responsibility was to earn a spot in the Europeans. If you're still around after that, of course, you can supervise the entire operation. The fact that I took a great deal of interest in the boys managing the minor teams during the several meetings we had gets lost in translation.

But, losing to Denmark was generally quite disheartening, and we then entered the Nations League, which was simply a series of inflated friendlies. The rules weren't known back then, and I don't believe they are known now either. The northern team's Michael O'Neill had the appropriate mindset from the start when he said that these games weren't significant.

The Northern Ireland supporters and, more importantly, the Northern Irish press recognized that as Michael's strategy.

— As the manager of Ireland, did you find Roy Keane to be a hassle? I recall that he had disagreements with Jonathan Walters and Harry Arter and that he released his book on the eve of an international game.

Roy will undoubtedly make headlines in some way, according to MO'N. You anticipated that his disagreements with Walters and Harry Arter would eventually slip out and make the headlines, especially in light of Stephen Ward's WhatsApp message.

These issues were more significant since Roy was present. I believed we could keep them on-site.

There aren't many football teams that I've played on where we haven't argued with each other at some point.

But as soon as Roy got engaged, they started making headlines. I never considered them to be significant,

significant happenings. I've always believed that we can defeat them in the end.

Yet, if you don't get a win right away, people will undoubtedly notice and comment, "Oh, there's tension in the air." I believe that if you asked players like Robbie Brady and Jeff Hendrick right now, they would tell you that their best moments in football were spent playing for the Republic of Ireland in the Euros.

— You write admiringly about your time spent in Celtic culture and how excellent Lobo Moravick was.

You bring up Moravick, who is without a doubt the best two-footed player I've ever worked with. When I joined the football team, he was around 33 years old; I preferred him to be 26 or 27. By the time we reached the Uefa Cup final [against Porto], he had already departed the team, but had he been 26 or 27 at the time instead of 33 or 34, he could have been able to create something in that 2003 final.

— **In what professional setting were you happiest?**

In all the locations I've gone to, I discovered a lot of satisfaction at the club level. For example, Wycombe Wanderers' players provided me with the chance to manage at a higher level. I owe them a lot because they gave the games their all. I had a terrific experience there as my kids were just starting to get older. After a rough start, Leicester City came out fantastic; I adored the team. Of course, Celtic was fantastic. Then, at Aston Villa, we had three top-six finishes. You mention having regrets.

I regret breaking up with Robert Chase at Norwich because I had two very brief playing stints there as well as a brief managerial stint. Therefore Norwich

City will always hold a special place in my heart. Of course, Celtic was fantastic, and according to my wife, Glasgow is her favorite city.

Billy Bingham names you captain of Northern Ireland in a fascinating paragraph in the book. The significance of this was not missed on either of you because you were a Catholic from Derry leading the squad. No one will care if we win games, Billy Bingham told you.

Billy is someone I owe a lot to. He might have chosen to ignore me for a simpler existence, but because of my time spent playing in Europe with Nottingham Forest and my experiences there, he thought I was a decent enough communicator. He went through with it even though he knew he would undoubtedly face criticism for it. And you're right; he said it will pass once we start winning football games. Hence, it was a brave choice.

— In a different reality, you might have spent a significant amount of time playing GAA for Derry if you hadn't managed to cross the water. You describe attending the 1958 All-Ireland final between Derry and Dublin and being there to watch your brother Leo play in the book.

I'm certain I would have played for Derry if I hadn't had the chance to travel over the river and play professional football. The future? We might have won the Ulster championship before moving on to the All-Ireland final. There was a noticeable undercurrent of envy for those boys who had achieved it when Derry did win it in 1993. The Sam Maguire Cup was brought to Derry, and that was a significant event. A major highlight for me would have been playing for Derry.

— During Euro 2016, I saw an article in which you claimed that losing the Hogan Cup final in 1970 was just as horrible as losing the Uefa Cup final with Celtic in 2003. That statement digs into your genetic makeup, the Gaelic heritage you carry, and how important it was to you when you were growing up.

Definitely. First of all, it would have been amazing for St. Malachy's to win the Hogan Cup because we had a tremendously strong team and should have easily defeated Coláiste Chrost R. of Cork in that match. I realized that you had to win and that these tales of bad luck don't matter at all. You must succeed. They nibble away at you because we lost in Croke Park and Seville.

— Have you ever seen a replay of Celtic's match against Porto in the 2003 Uefa Cup final?

I wouldn't, no. A few years ago, I watched it on television. They must have been in extra time and it must have been highlighted, so I just turned it off. Do you want to witness the highlights of Vitor Baia getting hurt, someone asked me. On that day, it is all too obvious. I can remember it without a TV.

— What was Henrik Larsson like? He went on to establish his value at Barcelona and Manchester United after Celtic. Do you believe that he improved with age?

I believe that is accurate because there was never in doubt that he would play up in Scotland, where he could only do it. Henrik Larsson excelled against Porto in the Uefa Cup final, one of several outstanding performances he made for Celtic.

He was a highly good player who was fearless and capable of scoring goals. When he comes on in the

2006 Champions League final [against Arsenal], he goes to Barcelona and helps flip the match, then in the closing stages of his career, he goes and scores goals for Manchester United. All of those things, in my opinion, demonstrate his ability to perform at the top level.

— You claim to be addicted to football, yet it's a job where loyalty isn't always present.

In my opinion, money has significantly altered many facets of football. When I played football, there was no power at all for the players, and that was unfair. Now, players hold all the power, which is unfair. So somewhere along the line, there must be a happy medium. I don't mind if great athletes like Messi and Ronaldo get money at all because they draw crowds to the stadium to see them play. People become upset when they hear about young athletes making money and then feeling entitled to it because it wasn't truly earned, in that case.

— Is there still a chance you'll succeed this time?

I'd not discount it. I believe that the game may be ageist. No job can be considered perfect. I don't have any employees, therefore you have to promote yourself, and for the past few years, I may have been hiding behind COVID. I would have to think carefully if they asked me to do something and an opportunity presented itself.

— Do you remain in contact with Roy Keane?

I do, on occasion. Fortunately, we didn't work together every day. He is traveling to the World Cup and is doing pretty well as a pundit. Maybe once a month, I'd communicate with him.

Printed in Great Britain
by Amazon

36725420R00050